Also by Bob Hartman:
The *Rhyming Parable Series*
Bob Hartman's Rhyming Bible
The Link-it-Up Bible
The Tell-it-Together Gospel
The Lion Storyteller Bible 25th Anniversary Edition
Welcome to the Journey
Where Do I Come from?

———————

First published in Great Britain in 2022

Society for Promoting Christian Knowledge
36 Causton Street, London SW1P 4ST
www.spck.org.uk

Text copyright © Bob Hartman 2019, 2022
Illustrations copyright © Mark Beech 2019, 2022

British Library Cataloguing-in-Publication Data
A catalogue record for this book is avaliable from the British Library

ISBN 978–0–281–08636–8

Printed by Imago

Produced on paper from sustainable forests

Bob Hartman's
RHYMING CHRISTMAS

Fantastic
illustrations by

Mark Beech

spck

A WOMAN CALLED MARY

A woman called Mary
Was doing her chores,
When an angel arrived,
But not through the doors.

He simply appeared
And she dropped to the floor.
'Hello, Mary', he said.
'GOD IS WITH YOU.'

'God is with me?' She wondered.
'But what does that mean?
What's this all about?
Is it some kind of dream?'
The angel just smiled.
'Don't be scared. Please don't scream.
God is happy with you
AND WILL BLESS YOU!'

God knocks down the proud,
And lifts up the meek,
And does mighty things
For those who are weak.
And blesses the ones
Whose service he seeks.

**SO SING OUT
HIS PRAISE,**

**HE'S
AMAZING!**

'You'll soon have a baby,'
The angel went on.
'A quite special baby
Called **JESUS**, God's Son.
The heir of King David,
He'll sit on his throne.
And his kingdom
WILL LAST FOR EVER.'

'But how?' Mary asked. 'I don't understand. I'm engaged to be wed But he's not yet my man.'

'Trust God,' said the angel. 'He's got it all planned. His Spirit will **COME UPON YOU.'**

God knocks down the proud, And lifts up the meek, And does mighty things For those who are weak. And blesses the ones Whose service he seeks.

SO SING OUT HIS PRAISE,

HE'S AMAZING!

'GOD'S OWN HOLY SON
Is the child you will bear.
IMPOSSIBLE? NO!
Your cousin would swear
That she can't have a baby,
The proof is right there.
She's expecting a son.
GO AND SEE HER.

'THERE'S NOTHING
THAT GOD
Cannot do, don't you see?'
'Well, then,' Mary nodded,
'Please do that for me,
This impossible thing.
His servant I'll be.'
Then the angel waved
'BYE'.
And he left her.

All night, Joseph tossed. All night, Joseph turned.
He just couldn't sleep. He'd only just learned
That Mary was pregnant. What's more, she'd confirmed
That the baby she bore was not his.

JOSEPH don't worry, JOSEPH don't weep.
Lay down your head, and go back to sleep.
Mary's been faithful. Her love's strong and deep,
And her baby is God's own son.

She'd told him this tale: an angelic visit,
A son to be born by God's Holy Spirit.
The more she went on, the less he believed it.
He wanted to break their engagement.

But just as sleep came, that angel appeared.
'Don't worry,' he said, 'there's nothing to fear.
I know that you're troubled, so you need to hear
That Mary is telling the truth.

'The baby she bears is God's holy son.
Call his name JESUS, for he is the one
God promised to send to save everyone.
IMMANUEL, GOD IS WITH US!'

'He's the answer to all that the prophets have said.
So keep your engagement. Be glad and be wed.'
And when Joseph woke up, that's just what he did.
He took Mary to be his wife.

JOSEPH don't worry, JOSEPH don't weep.
Lay down your head, and go back to sleep.
Mary's been faithful. Her love's strong and deep,
And her baby is God's own son.

COUNTING NUMBERS

'How many people live in my land?'
The ruler of Rome asked, one day.
'Let's have a big count!' he said to his men.
"And let's do it right away!'

Out of the blue, the order was given.
All through the world it went round.
To make the maths easy, they told everyone
To go back to their hometown.

So even though Joseph
lived Nazareth way,
A village right up in the **NORTH**,
His family came from Bethlehem town.
So down to the south he set **FORTH**.

He set forth with Mary
his quite pregnant wife,
A ninety-mile journey to clock.
And though you might think
that she rode on a donkey
It's more likely that they walked!

Several weeks later,
they showed up in town,
Looking for somewhere to stay
"BETHLEHEM'S FULL!"
"NO VACANCIES HERE!"
And everyone sent them away.

Then one caring cousin
came up with a plan.
"Our guest room is full," he shared.
"But in the front room
where the animals stay,
There's plenty of space to spare!"

So Mary gave birth to God's promised son
In a room filled with cows and with sheep.
She wrapped him in cloths, and there in a manger
Made him a place to sleep.

Now, count all the countries in Caesar's Empire
And all the roads Mary trod.
Add 'no-spaces-places', the number you get
Is **ONE** special Son of God!

IT BEGINS IN BETHLEHEM.

Shepherds lying on a hill.
The night was silent, all was still.
They watched their flock of grazing sheep,
And tried hard not to fall asleep.

When, **BRIGHT** and white, an angel came
to light the night, a fiery flame.
The shepherds trembled where they lay.
The angel said, 'Don't be afraid.'

Sing praise to God and give him glory.
Celebrate his wondrous story
Of love and joy and peace to men,
For it begins in **BETHLEHEM.**

'The news is good, the news I bring.
GOOD NEWS to make you leap and sing.
GOOD NEWS for people everywhere.
GOOD NEWS of joy for all to share.

'Good news, for God has kept his word,
And sent his saviour, Christ the Lord.
The one he promised he would send
Is born this day in BETHLEHEM.'

'And this will be a sign for you.
This is how you'll know it's true.
You'll find a BABY wrapped in cloth,
Sleeping in a cattle trough.'

The angel, then, was joined by more,
Six and twelve and twenty-four,
And then too many more to number,
A heaven-choir, **LOUD AS THUNDER**.

And so the angels left that place,
Just like they'd come, without a trace,
Except for all they sang and said,
Which echoed in the shepherds' heads.

'Let's go to Bethlehem and see,'
The shepherds all, as one, agreed.
They found the baby where he lay,
Asleep upon a bed of hay.

They told them what the angels said.
Then Mary smiled and raised her head.
A secret hid there, in her eyes,
For she was not one bit surprised.

So back they went to sheep and hill,
No longer silent, hardly still,
But singing loud like angels bright
Of all that they had seen that night.

Sing praise to **GOD** and give him glory,
Celebrate his wondrous story
Of love and joy and peace to men,
For it begins in BETHLEHEM.

ONE HUMP, TWO HUMPS

The star-watchers watched the stars go by,
Looking for secrets in the sky.
And then they saw a special star,
Away in the west. Away off far.

'A king's been born! That's what it means.
Judea way, or so it seems.'
They climbed aboard their camel-y beasts
And set off west from their homes back east.

One **HUMP**, two **HUMPS**, lumpety-lump,
The star-watchers went with a **BUMP** and a **THUMP**.
One **HUMP**, two **HUMPS**, lumpety-lump,
The star-watchers followed the star.

At last their journey came to an end.
They parked their camels in Jerusalem.
They went to **HEROD**, king of the nation,
To ask him for some information.

'Oh king,' they asked. They were quite polite.
'Somewhere, round here, on this starry night,
A brand new **BABY KING** abides.
Can you tell us where this child resides?'

A worried look crossed Herod's face.
He had no plans to be replaced.
So he asked his priests if they could tell
Where this brand new baby king might dwell.

The priests all answered straight away.
'BETHLEHEM is what the prophets say.'
Then Herod thought an evil thing.
'I think I need to meet this king.'

'Star-watchers, friends,' King Herod smiled.
'In Bethlehem you'll find the child.
Would you tell me where you find him, please?
The exact address would put my mind at ease.'

Herod, of course, told them a LIE.
He'd already planned for the child to DIE.
When he found the boy, that's what he'd do.
So the star-watchers left, without a clue.

The shining star led them to the place.
A simple house, not some fancy space.
And when they saw the little boy,
They gave him a pile of special 'toys'.

Presents, rather, fit for a king.
A bunch of shiny **GOLDEN THINGS**.
A spice called **MYRRH**, a sort of perfume.
While smelly **FRANKINCENSE** filled the room.

Then, in the night, they had a dream
That showed them Herod's evil scheme.
So they didn't say where the boy's house lay
But went straight home by another way.

One **HUMP**, two **HUMPS**, lumpety-lump,
The star-watchers went with a **BUMP** and a **THUMP**.
One **HUMP**, two **HUMPS**, lumpety-lump,
The star-watchers followed the star.

A PRESENT
FOR YOU

'So what is the point of angels and shepherds
And camels and stars?' you say.
'Is it just a nice story to tell to the children
To celebrate **CHRISTMAS DAY**?'

It's not just a story. It's not just for kids.
It's the hinge on which history swings!
That Bethlehem baby grew into a man
Who challenged all powers and kings.

He taught us that LOVE is better than hate,
That serving beats being in charge.
He showed us the value of each human life:
The little as well as the large.

And then, on a cross he died for us,

Died to take all our wrongs away.

And walked, three days later, right out of his tomb

To turn death's dark night to day.

And that is the good news the angels proclaimed:

The heart of all Jesus would do.

A new life for now. A new life forever.

**THAT'S HIS CHRISTMAS PRESENT
TO YOU!**

HOW MANY OF ME CAN YOU SEE?

How many angels, sheep and mice can you spot throughout the story?

ANSWERS:
24 angels, 16 sheep, 10 mice.